W9-AAZ-489

WITHDRAWN

WEATHER Infographics

Chris Oxlade

Raintree
Chicago, Illinois

© 2014 Raintree
an imprint of Capstone Global Library, LLC
Chicago, Illinois

To contact Capstone Global Library, please call 800-747-4992, or visit our web site www.capstonepub.com

All rights reserved. No part of this publication may be reproduced or transmitted in any form or by any means, electronic or mechanical, including photocopying, recording, taping, or any information storage and retrieval system, without permission in writing from the publisher.

Edited by Rebecca Rissman, Dan Nunn, and John-Paul Wilkins
Designed by Philippa Jenkins
Original illustrations © Capstone Global Library Ltd 2014
Illustrations by HL Studios
Picture research by Elizabeth Alexander
Production by Vicki Fitzgerald
Originated by Capstone Global Library Ltd
Printed in the United States of America in North Mankato, Minnesota.
052014 008243RP

17 16 15 14 13
10 9 8 7 6 5 4 3 2 1

Library of Congress Cataloging-in-Publication Data
Oxlade, Chris.
Weather / Chris Oxlade.
pages cm.—(Infographics)
Includes bibliographical references and index.
ISBN 978-1-4109-6219-5 (hardback)—ISBN 978-1-4109-6224-9 (paperback) 1. Graphic methods—Juvenile literature. 2. Charts, diagrams, etc.—Juvenile literature. 3. Weather—Juvenile literature. 4. Meteorology—Juvenile literature. I. Title.
QA90.O959 2014
551.6072'8—dc23 2013012536

Acknowledgments
We would like to thank the following for permission to reproduce photographs: Capstone Global Library p. 4; Shutterstock pp. 4 (© M.Stasy, © Pakhnyushcha, © Stella Caraman, © Thomas Bethge), 8 (© Alhovik), 9 (© Smit).

We would like to thank Diana Bentley and Marla Conn for their invaluable help in the preparation of this book.

Every effort has been made to contact copyright holders of any material reproduced in this book. Any omissions will be rectified in subsequent printings if notice is given to the publisher.

Disclaimer
All the Internet addresses (URLs) given in this book were valid at the time of going to press. However, due to the dynamic nature of the Internet, some addresses may have changed, or sites may have changed or ceased to exist since publication. While the author and publisher regret any inconvenience this may cause readers, no responsibility for any such changes can be accepted by either the author or the publisher.

Metric Conversions

Length and distance
1 millimeter = 0.04 inch
1 centimeter = 0.4 inch
1 foot = 0.3 meter
1 kilometer = 0.6 mile

Speed
1 kilometer per hour = 0.6 mile per hour

Weight
1 kilogram = 2.2 pounds
1 metric ton = 1.1 tons

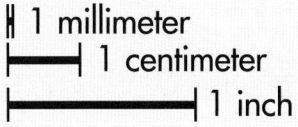

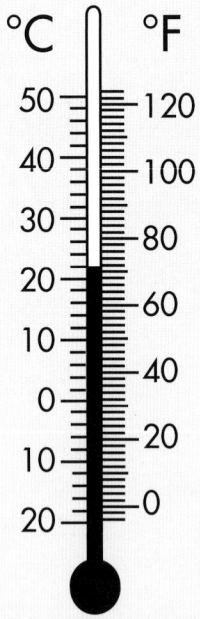

CONTENTS

About Infographics 4
What is Weather? 6
Temperature 8
Types of Weather 10
Clouds 16
Extreme Weather 20
Climates 24
Weather Forecasting 28
Glossary *30*
Find Out More *31*
Index *32*

Some words are shown in bold, **like this**. You can find out what they mean by looking in the glossary.

ABOUT INFOGRAPHICS

An infographic is a picture that gives you information. Infographics can be graphs, charts, maps, or other sorts of pictures. The infographics in this book are about weather.

Infographics make information easier to understand. We see infographics all over the place, every day. They appear in books, in newspapers, on television, on web sites, on posters, and in advertisements.

Weather for the week

Here is an example of a weather infographic. It shows what the weather might be like for the next week in a particular place.

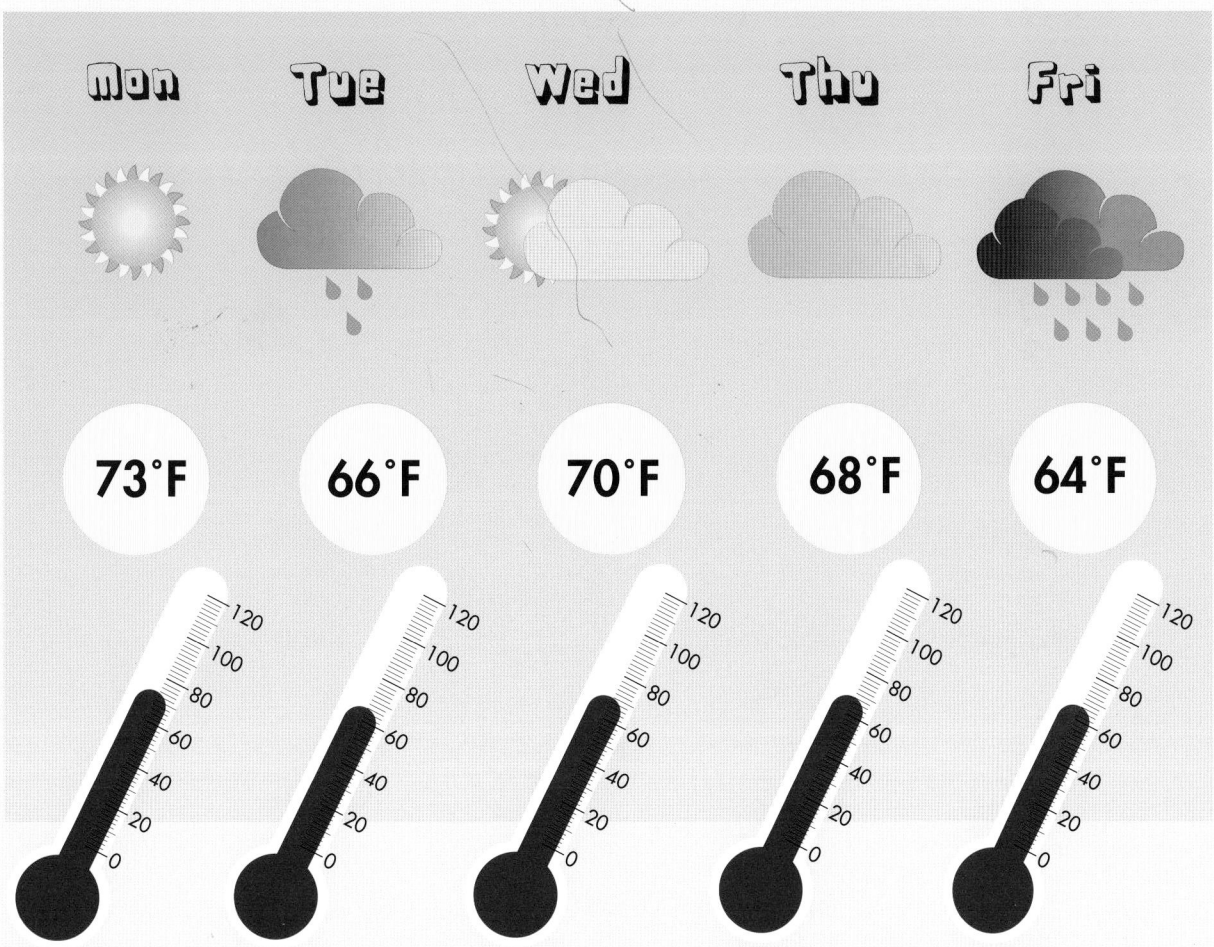

WHAT IS WEATHER?

Weather can be sunny or cloudy, wet or dry, warm or cold, or windy or **calm**. It can also be a mixture of lots of these things! We use different symbols to show different types of weather.

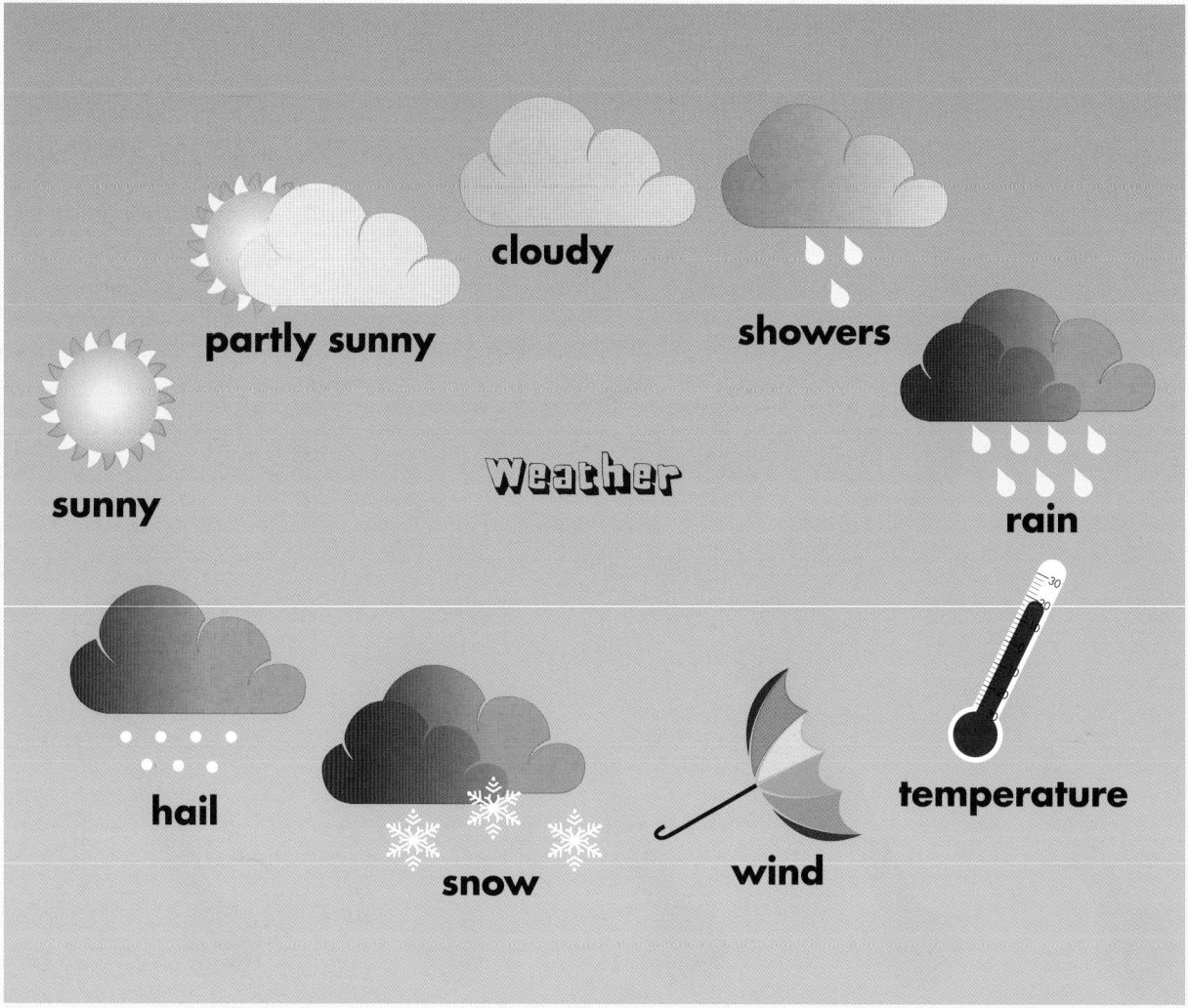

World record weather

Some places in the world are very hot or very cold. Some are very wet and some are very dry. Some are very windy. This map shows some world-record weather around the world.

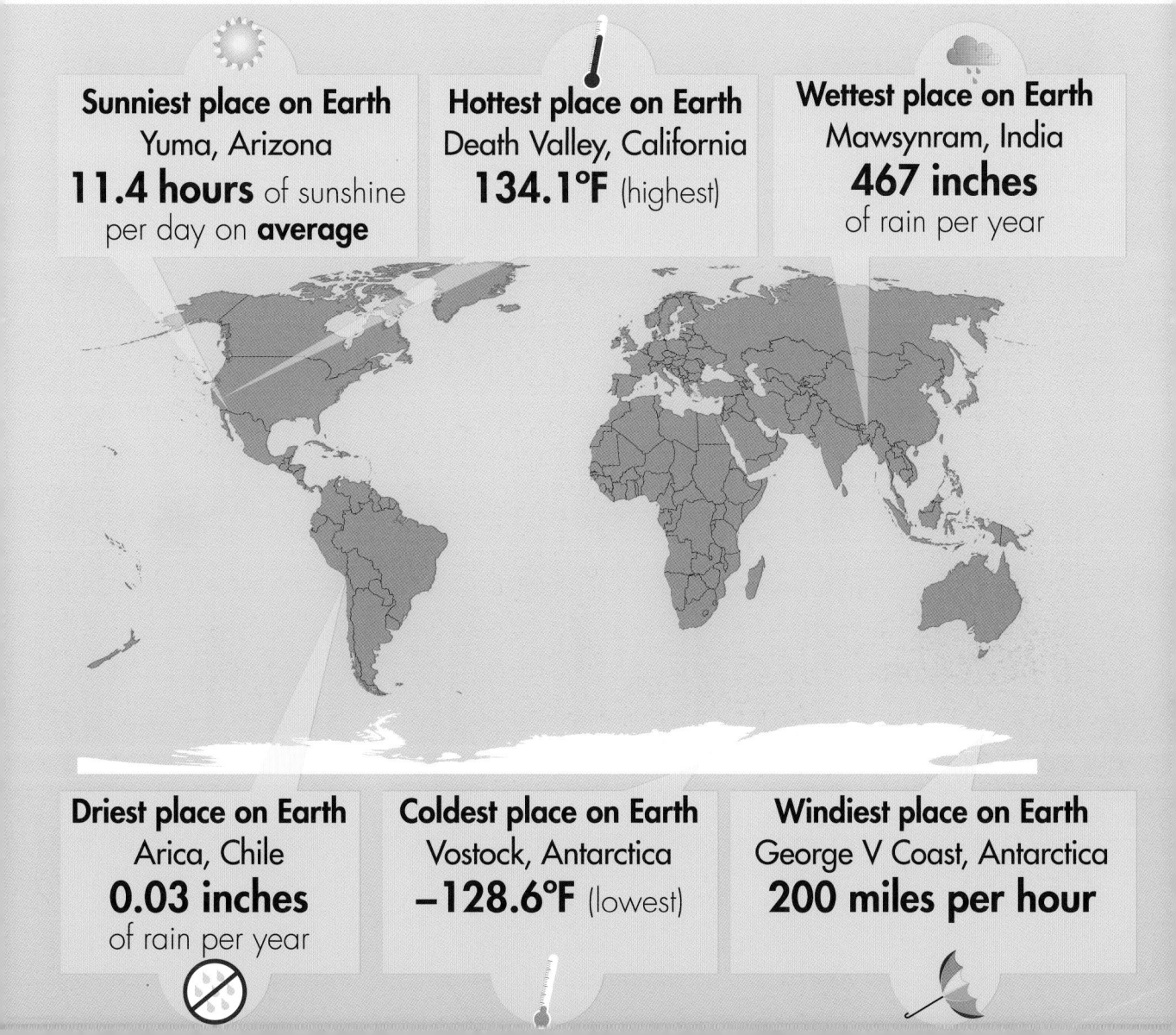

TEMPERATURE

How warm today?

Weather experts record the **temperature** regularly throughout the day and night. This is an example of a 24-hour temperature record. It shows how hot or cold it was every three hours, from midday on February 1 to midday on February 2, 2012, in Pittsburgh, Pennsylvania.

Temperature in degrees Fahrenheit

12 p.m.	3 p.m.	6 p.m.	9 p.m.	12 a.m.	3 a.m.	6 a.m.	9 a.m.	12 p.m.
52°F	**55.9°F**	**53.1°F**	**45°F**	**39°F**	**36°F**	**36°F**	**36°F**	**39.9°F**

How warm this week?

Weather experts record the weather all over the world every day. This graph shows the average temperature in London, England, on each day for a week in September 2012.

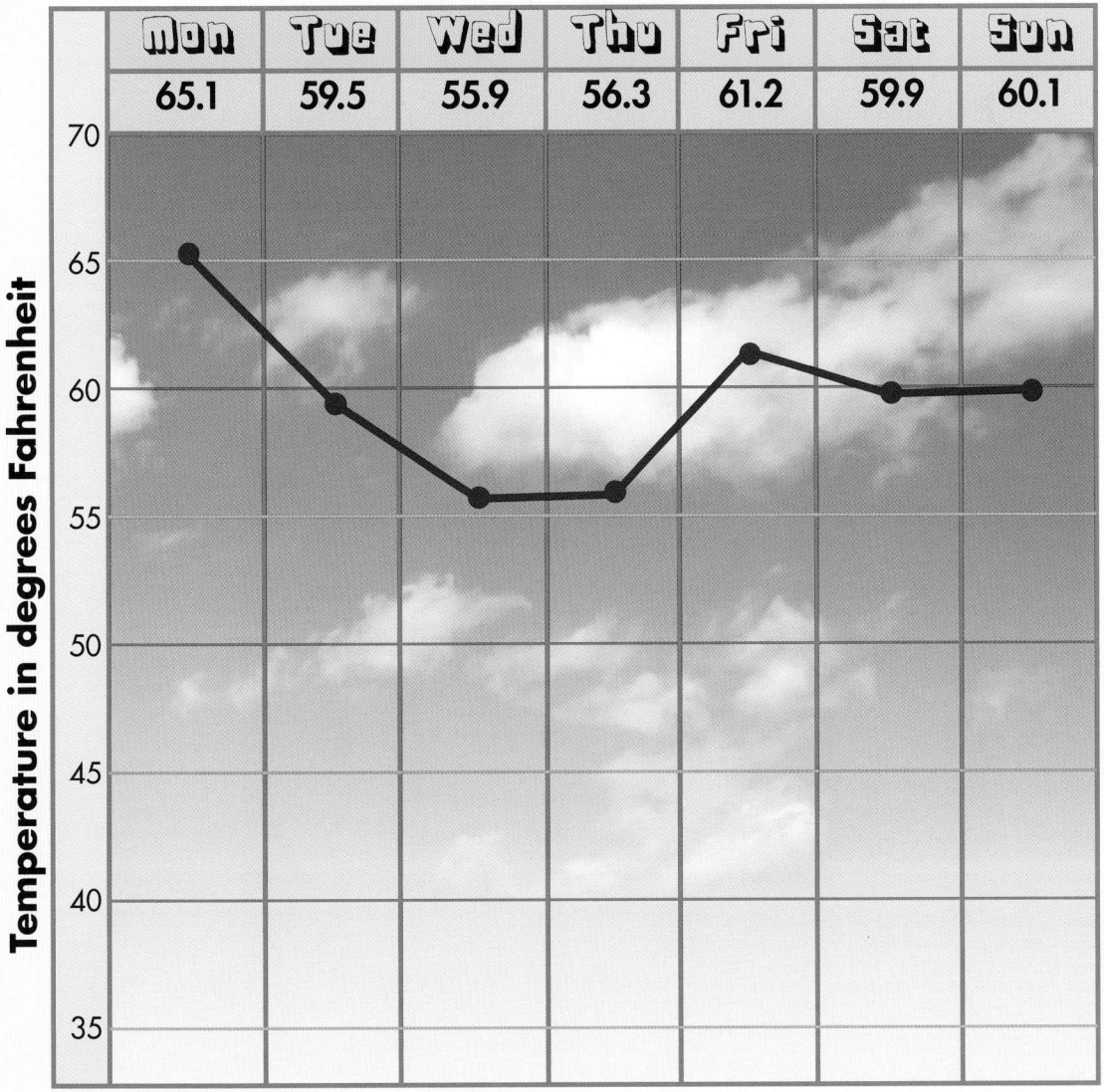

TYPES OF WEATHER

How much rain this week?

This is an example of a weekly rainfall chart. It shows how much rain fell each day for a week.

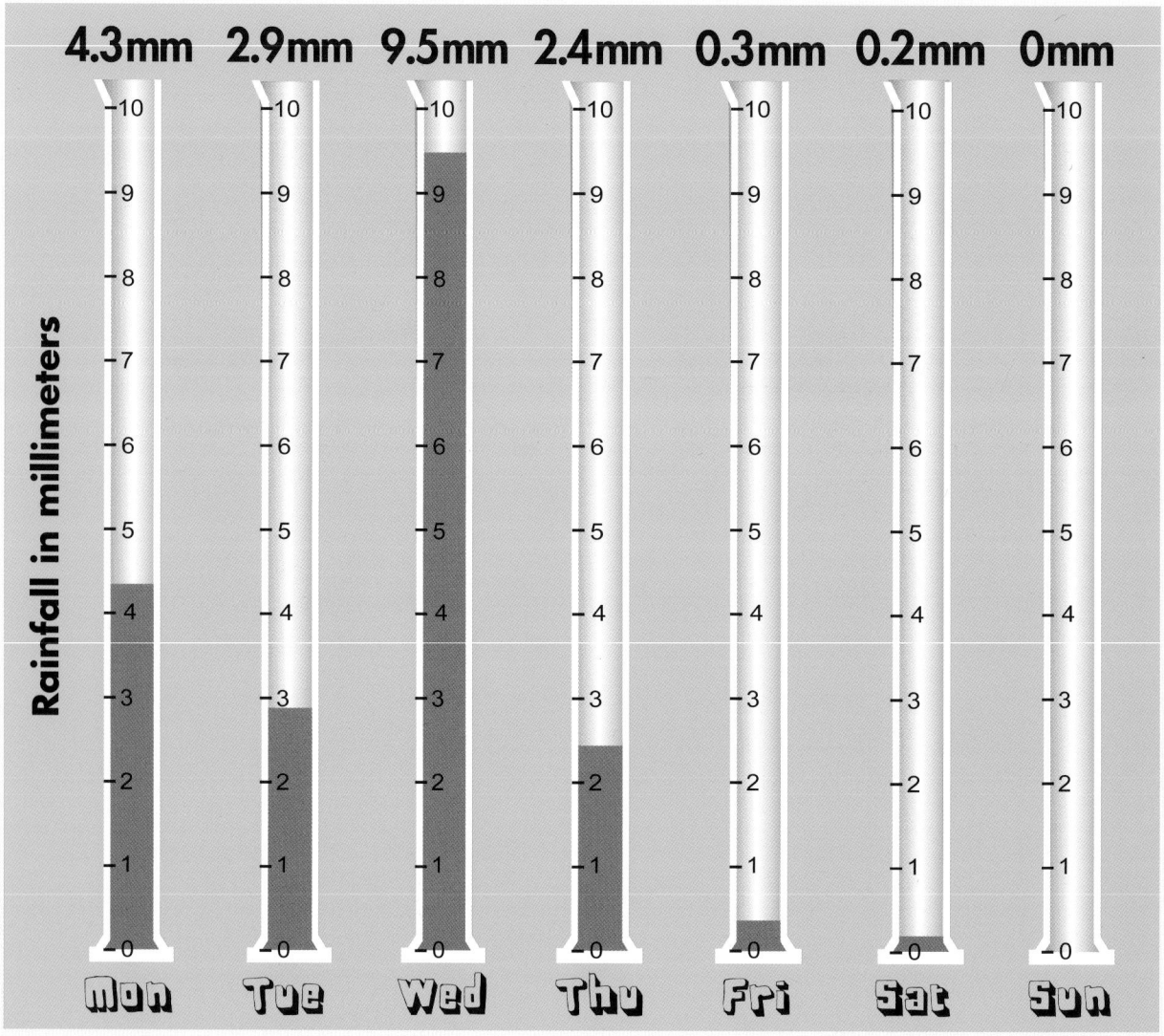

The heaviest rain

Sometimes it rains very heavily. This chart shows some of the heaviest downpours ever.

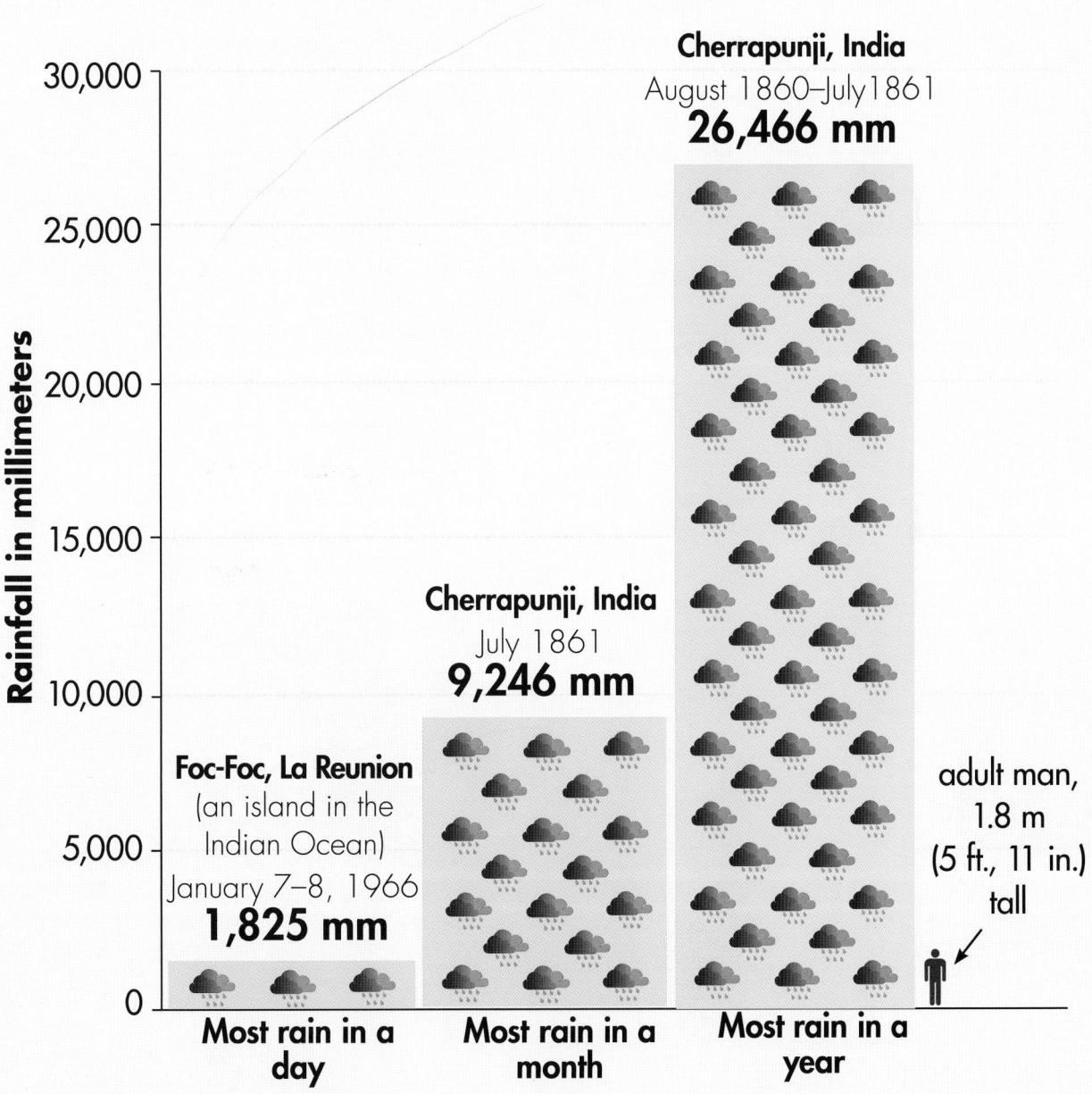

The biggest hail

Hail is made up of lumps of ice that fall from clouds. The lumps are called hailstones. Some hailstones are enormous. This map shows where some of the worst hailstorms have taken place.

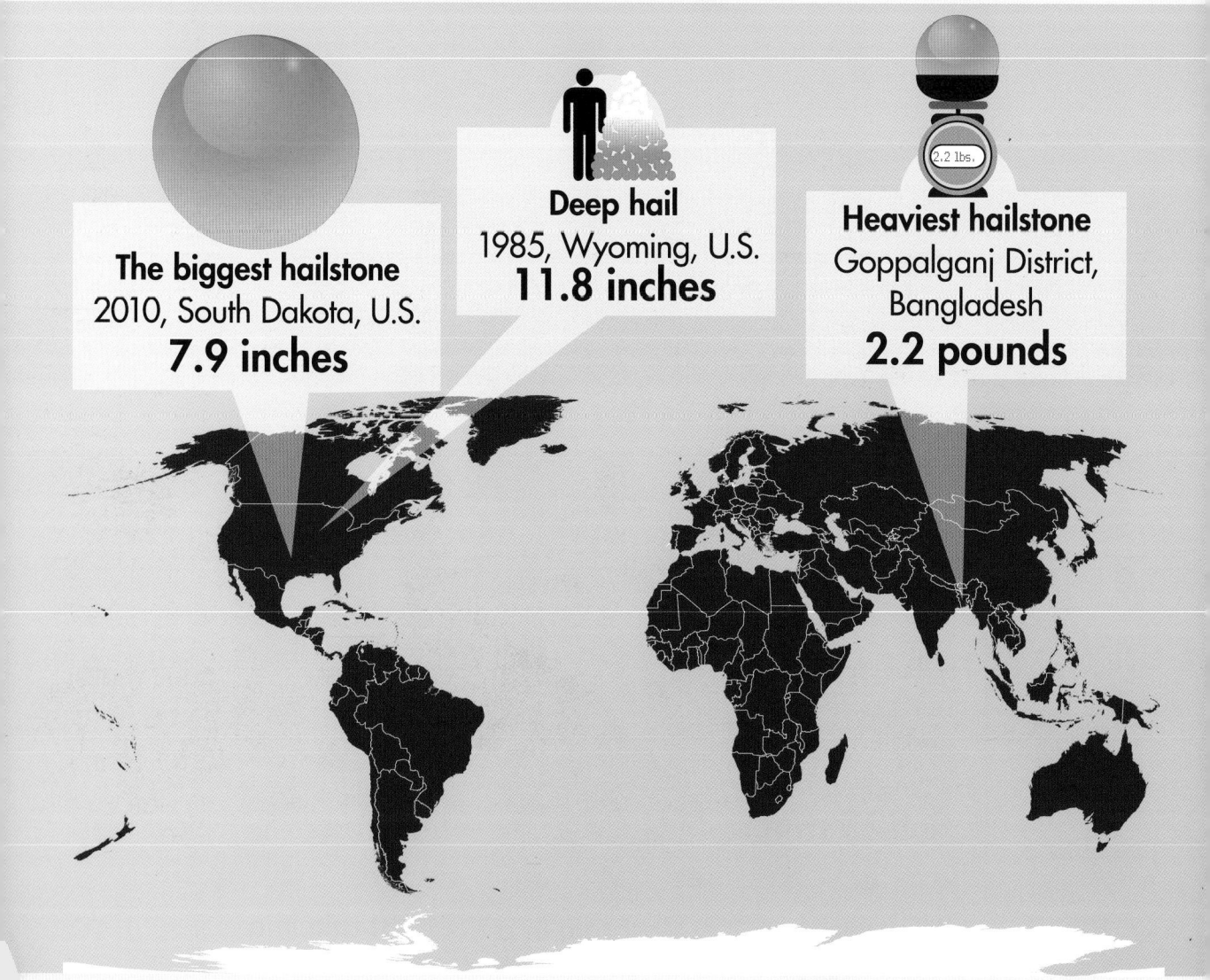

How snowy?

The amount of snow that falls is measured by how deep the snow gets on the ground. This chart shows the amount of snow that fell each month in Banff, Canada, in 2006.

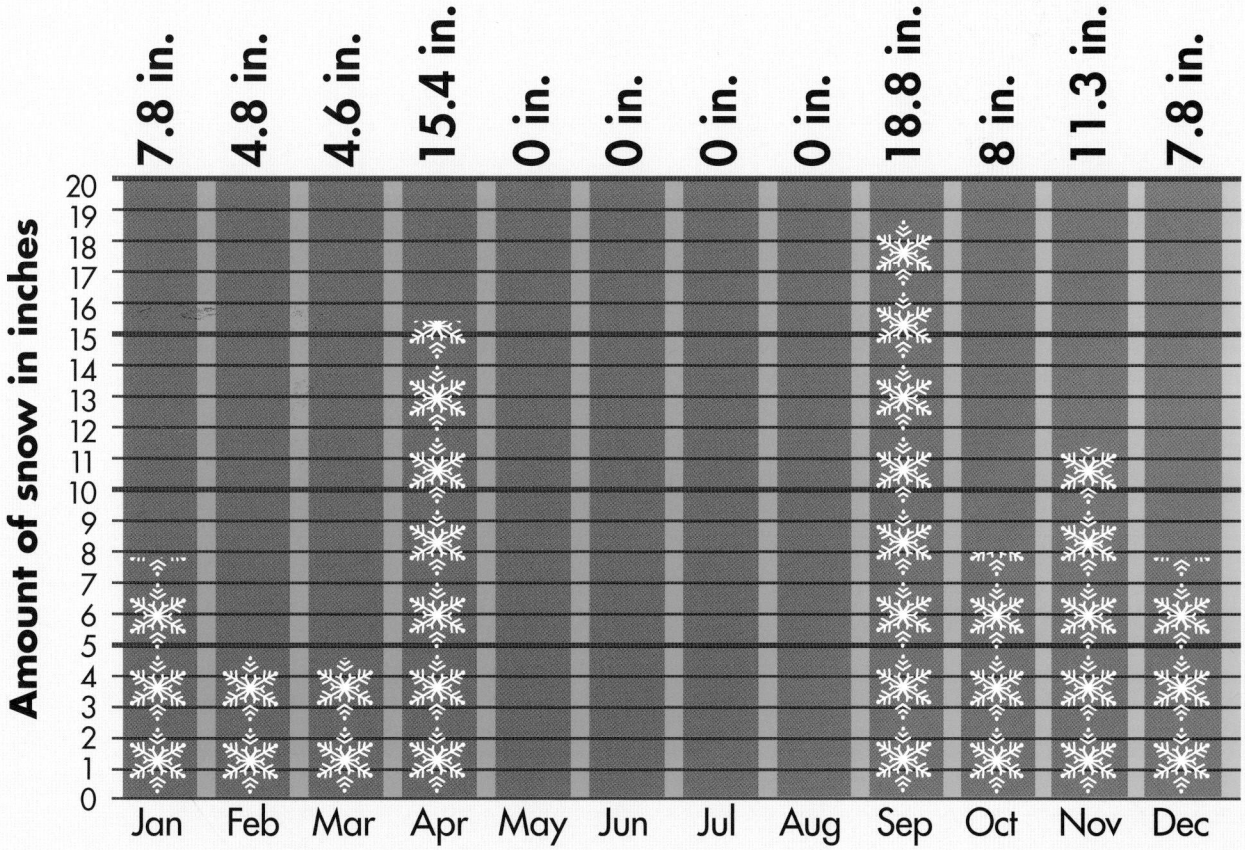

How windy?

Weather experts measure two things about the wind. They measure the strength of the wind and which way the wind is blowing. This chart shows how the strength and direction of the wind at Sydney Airport, Australia, changed during a day.

We show wind speed in miles per hour (mph). At **9 a.m.** the strength was **11 mph**

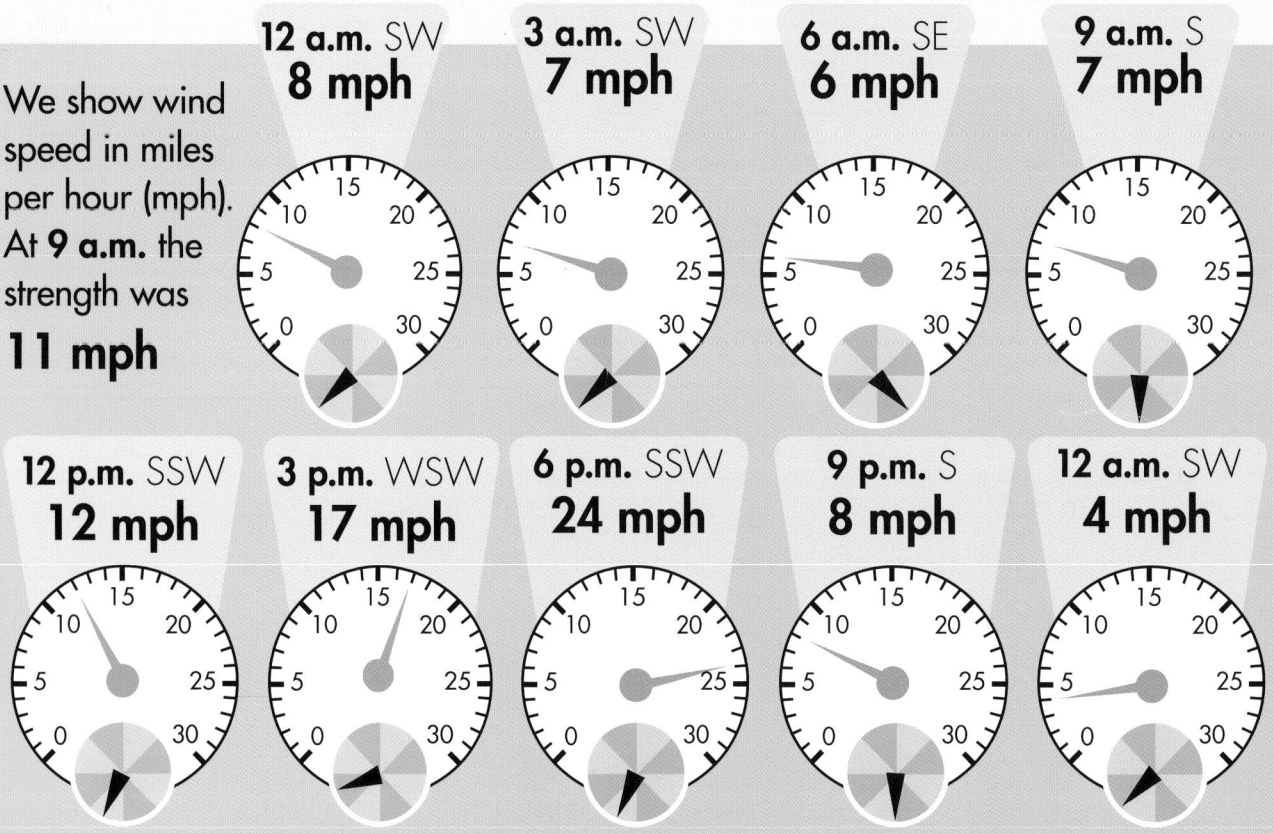

We show wind direction with the points of a **compass**. At **9 a.m.** the wind was blowing from north to south.

How sunny?

This is an example of a sunshine chart. It shows how many hours of sunshine there were each day for a week.

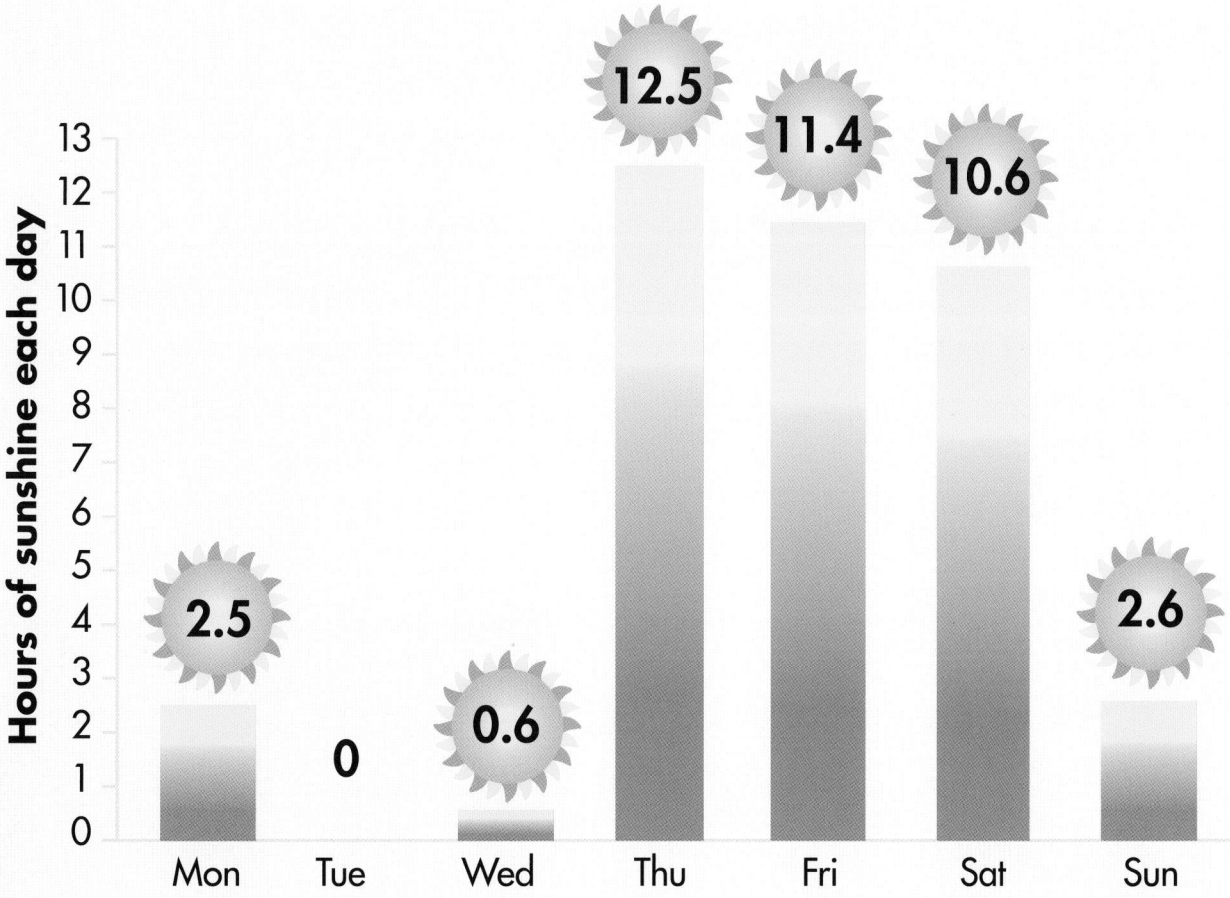

CLOUDS

Cloud shapes and sizes

Clouds come in many different shapes and sizes. This chart shows some of the clouds you might see when you look at the sky.

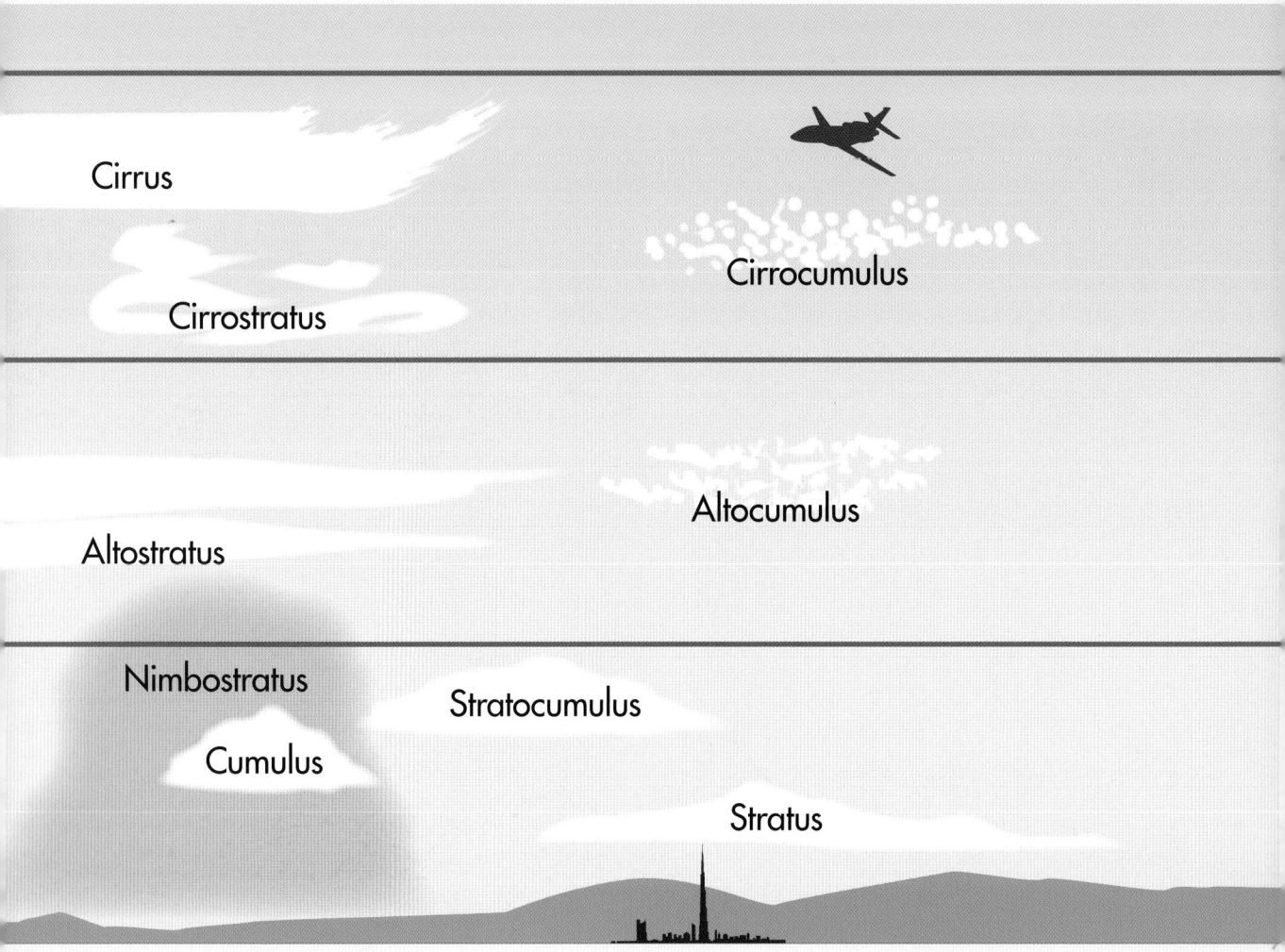

Clouds are named by their shape and how high in the sky they are.

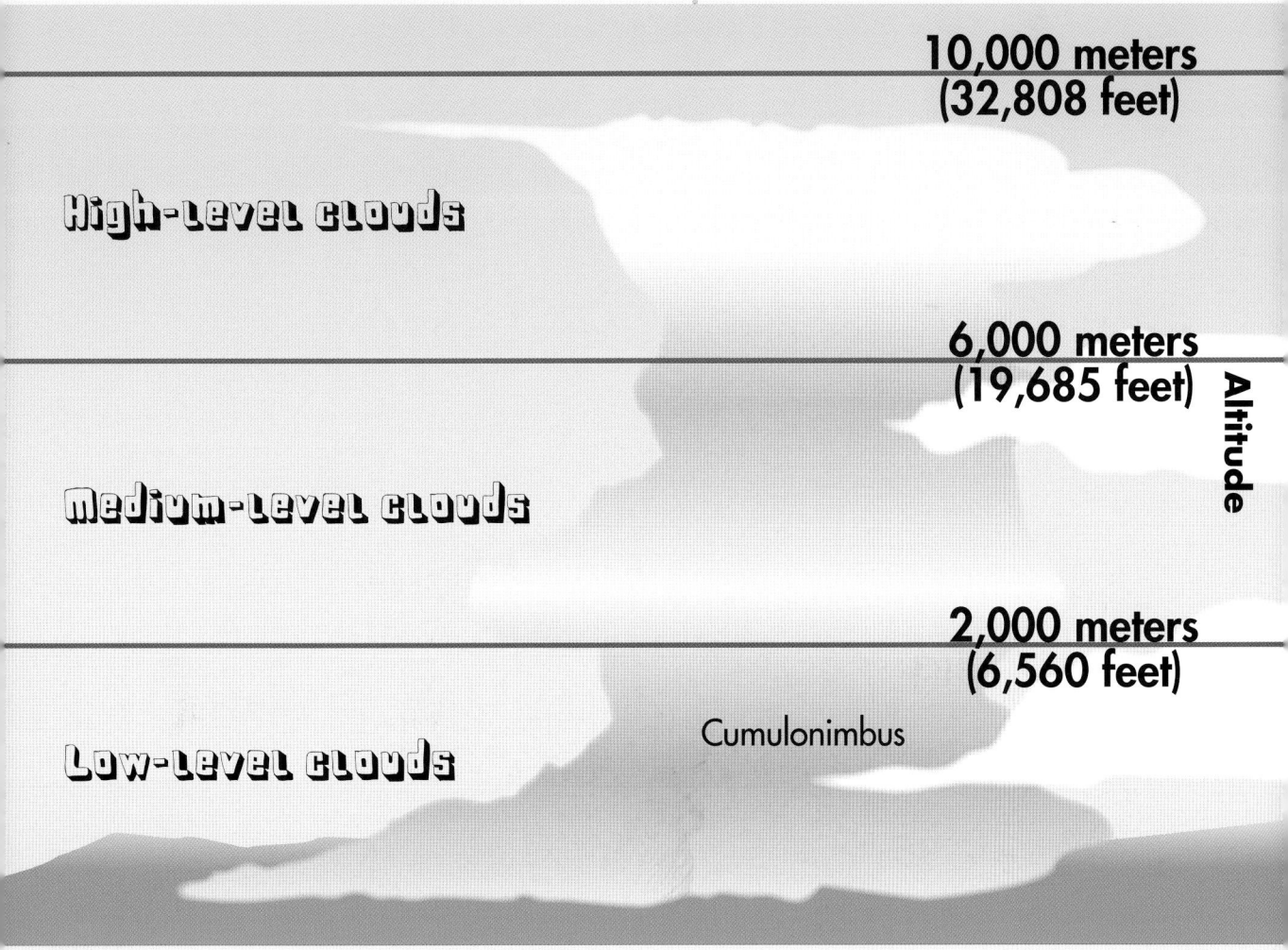

Thunder and lightning facts

Thunderstorms are giant clouds full of electricity. This infographic is about **thunder** and **lightning**.

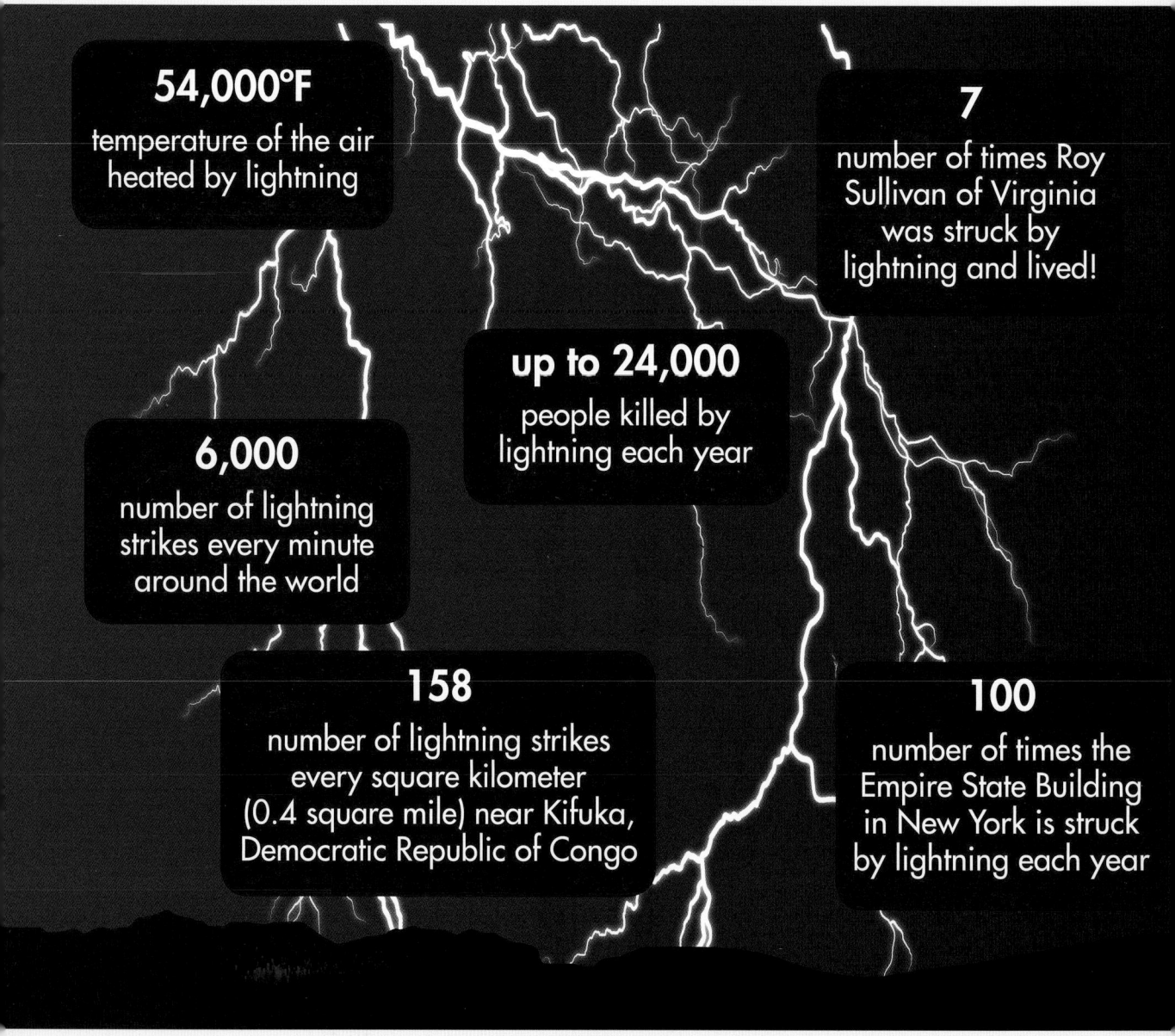

Thunder map

This map shows which areas of the world get the most thunderstorms.

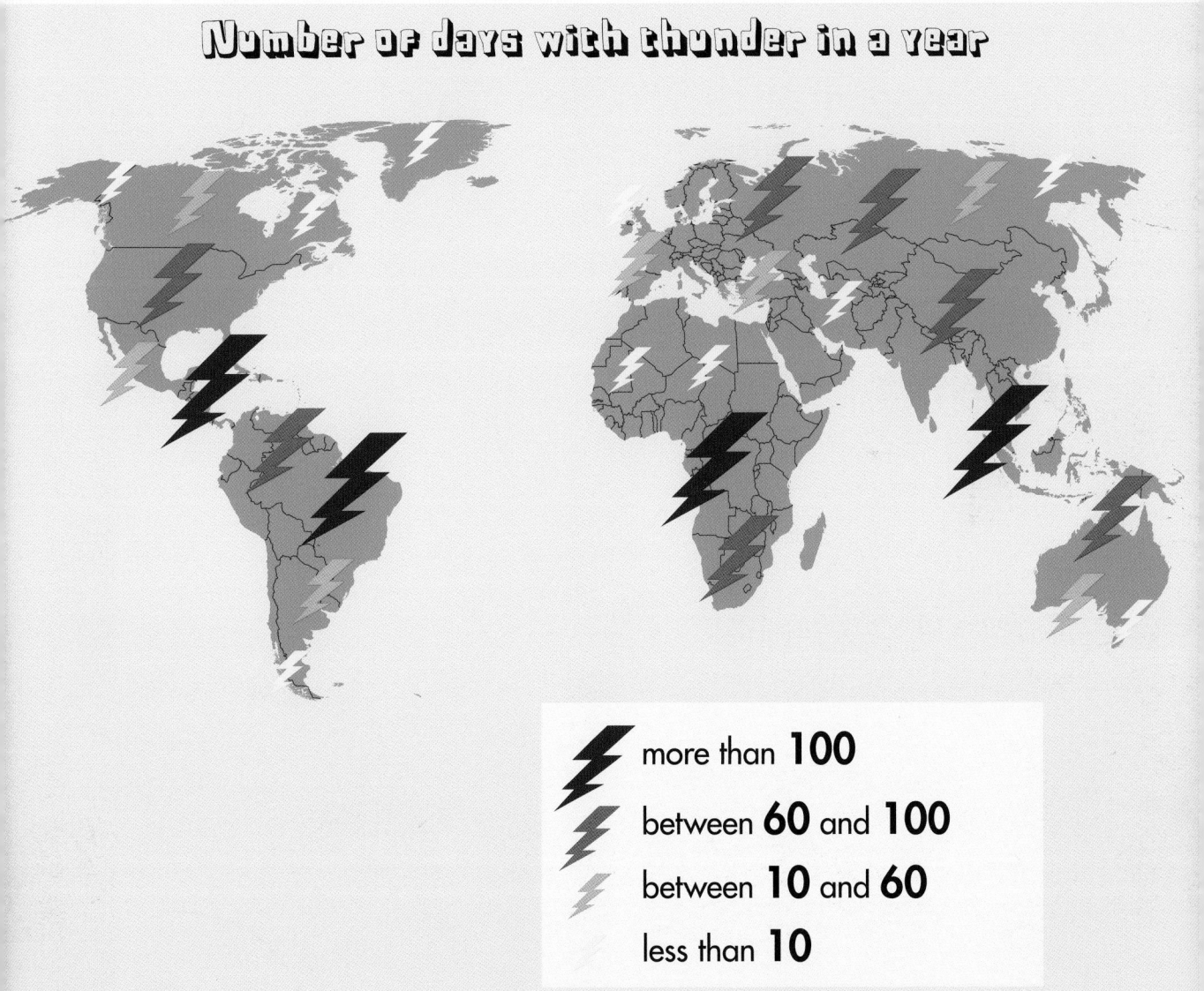

EXTREME WEATHER

Hurricanes

A hurricane is a giant swirling storm. Hurricanes start over the sea and sometimes hit land. They can cause terrible destruction. This infographic is about hurricanes.

A hurricane from above

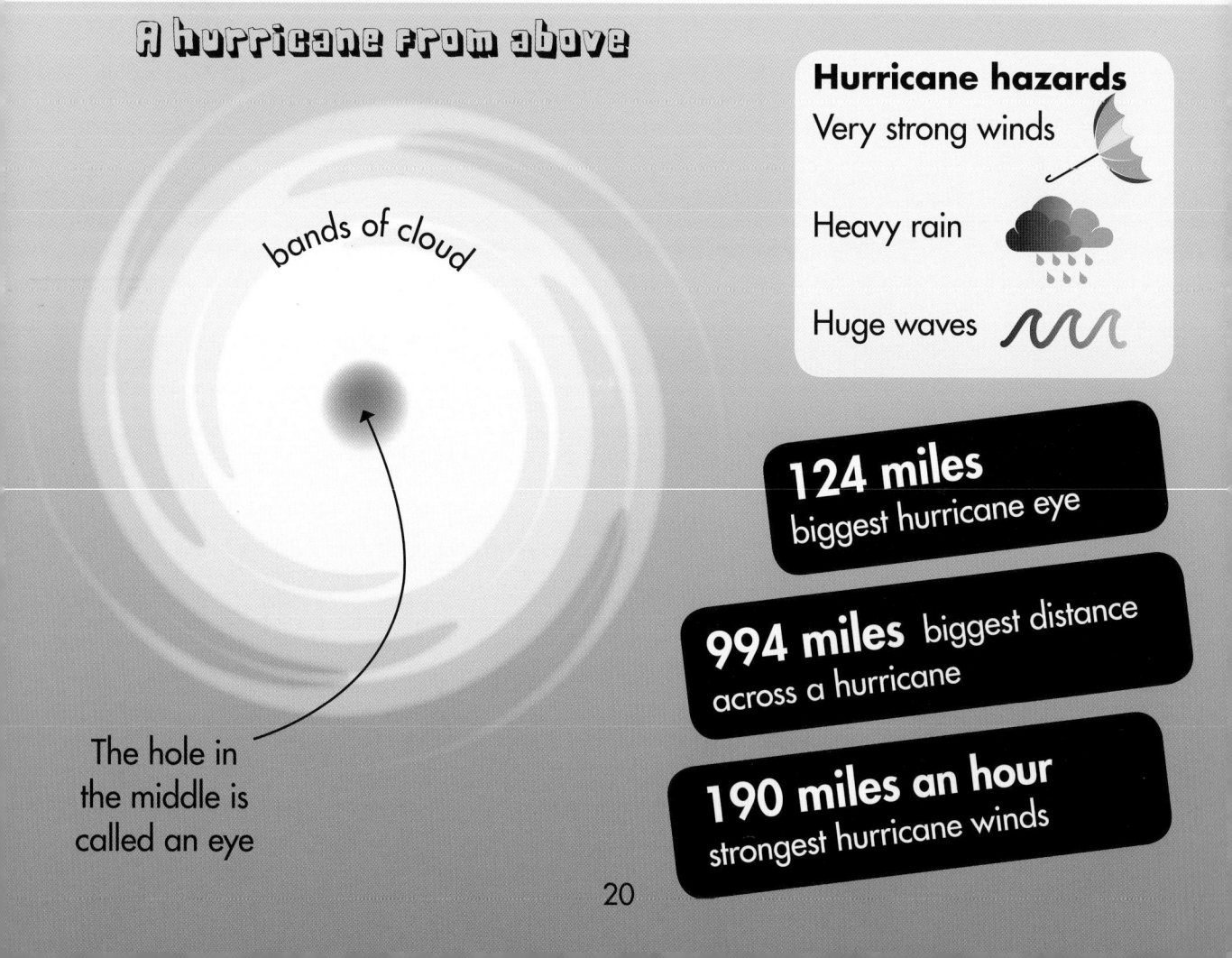

Where hurricanes strike

Hurricanes are called cyclones and typhoons in some parts of the world. They form near the equator. This map shows where hurricanes start and the paths they follow.

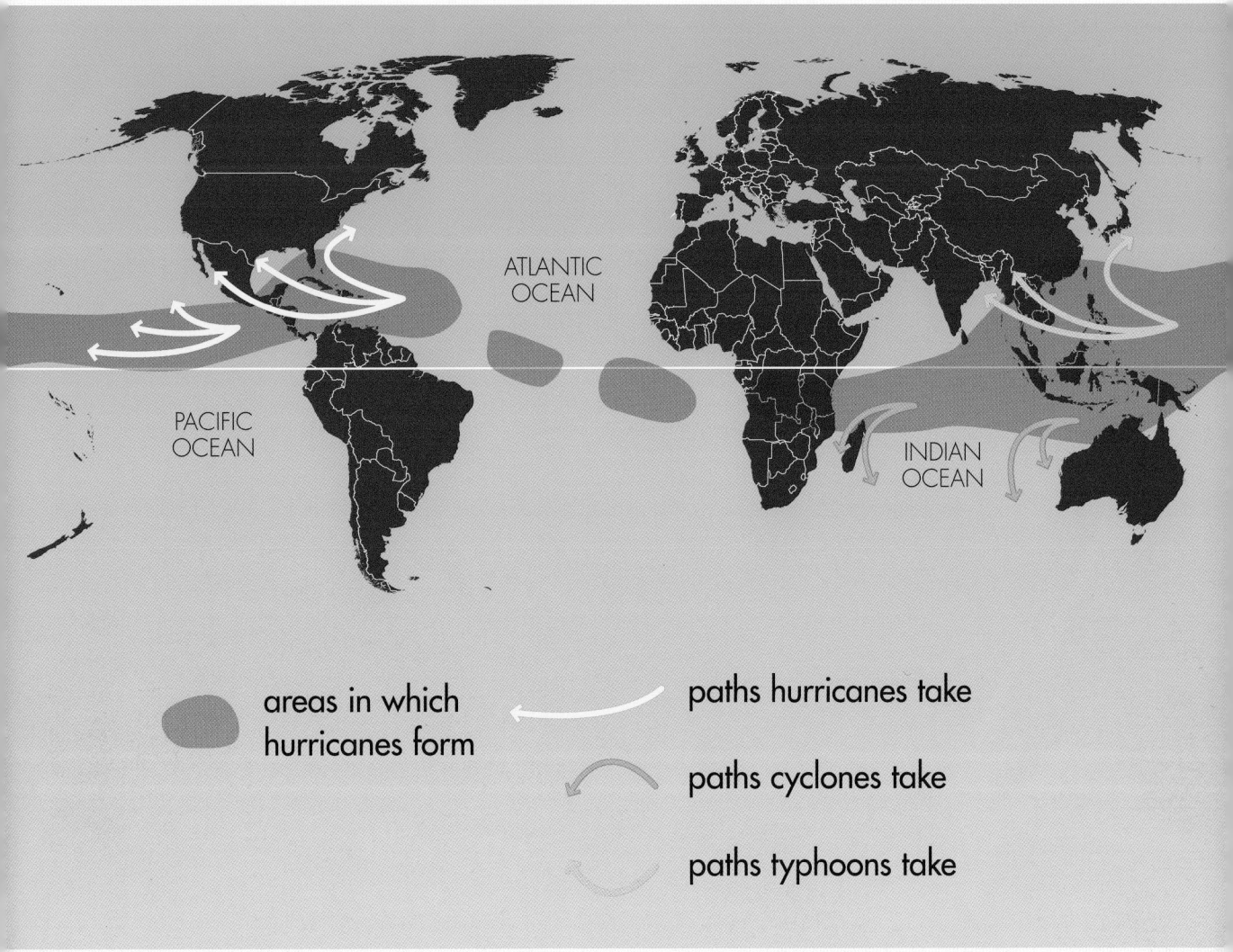

Tornado facts

This infographic is about tornadoes. A tornado is a funnel-shaped storm. It spins very fast, making super strong winds. Tornadoes always hang down from giant thunderstorms.

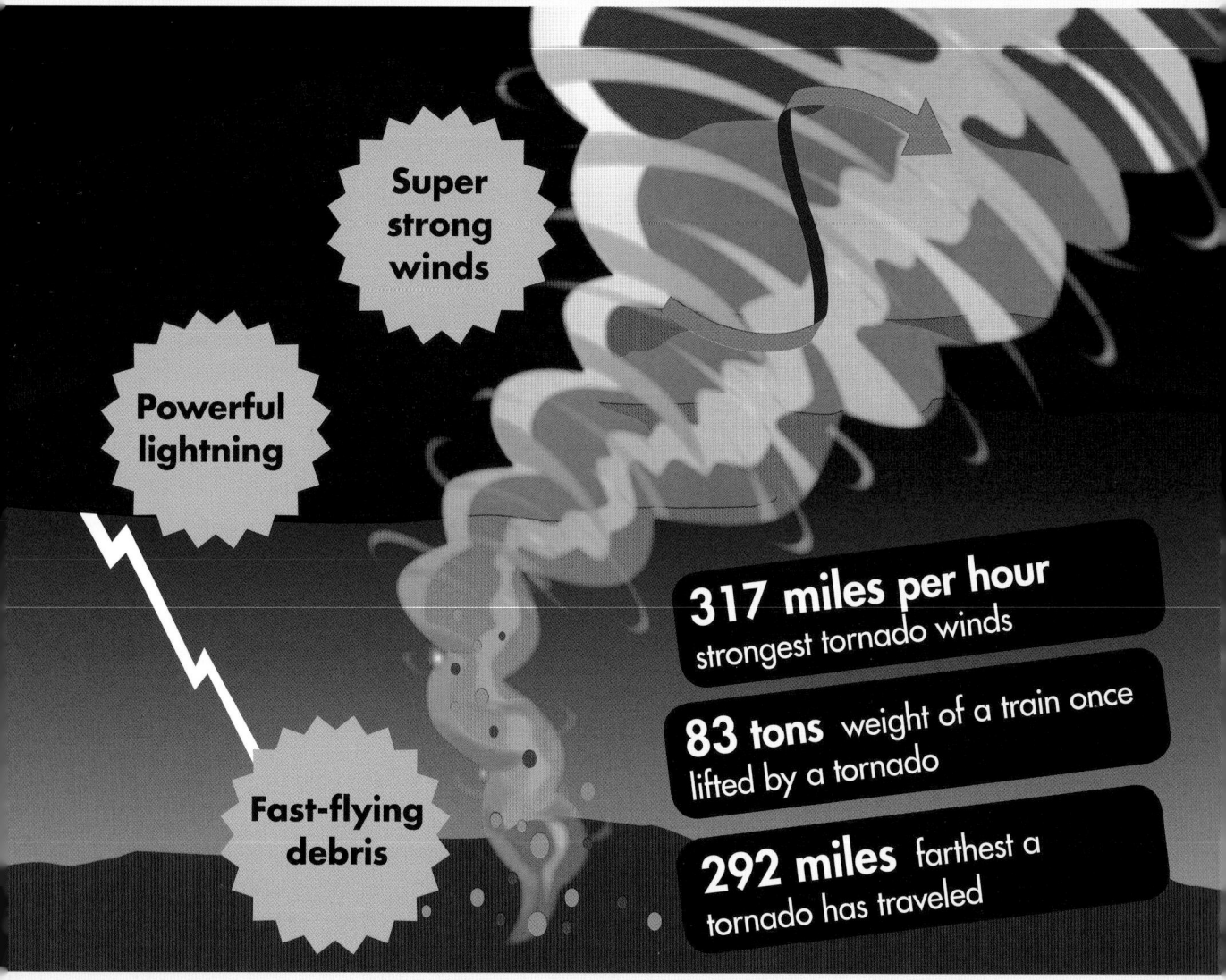

Tornado Alley

Tornadoes happen in many places around the world, but the most famous place is an area of the United States known as Tornado Alley. This map shows where Tornado Alley is.

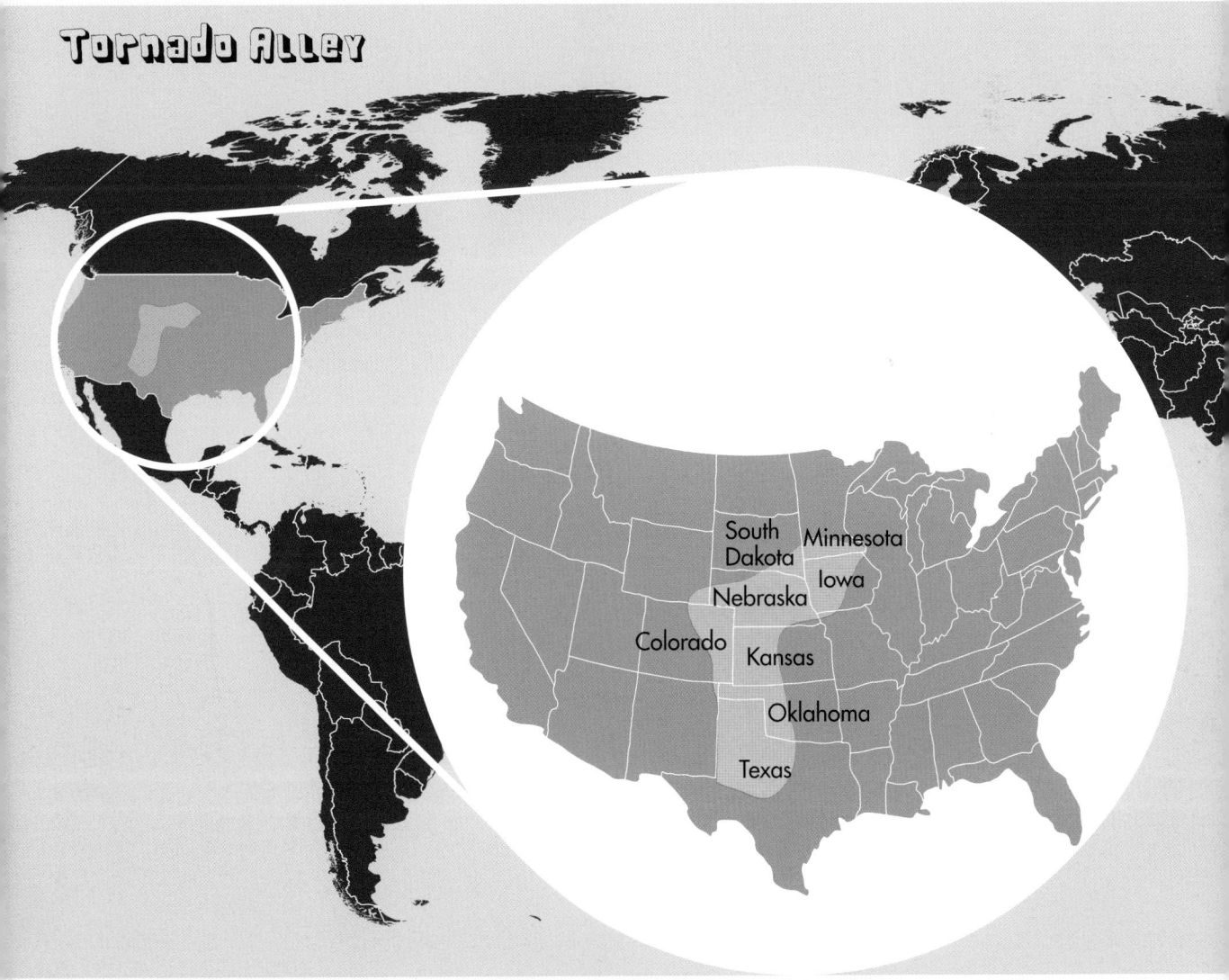

CLIMATES

Climate is the pattern of weather over time. We show climates by how much rain falls during a year, and what the temperature is over a year. This chart shows how much rain normally falls each month of the year in a certain place.

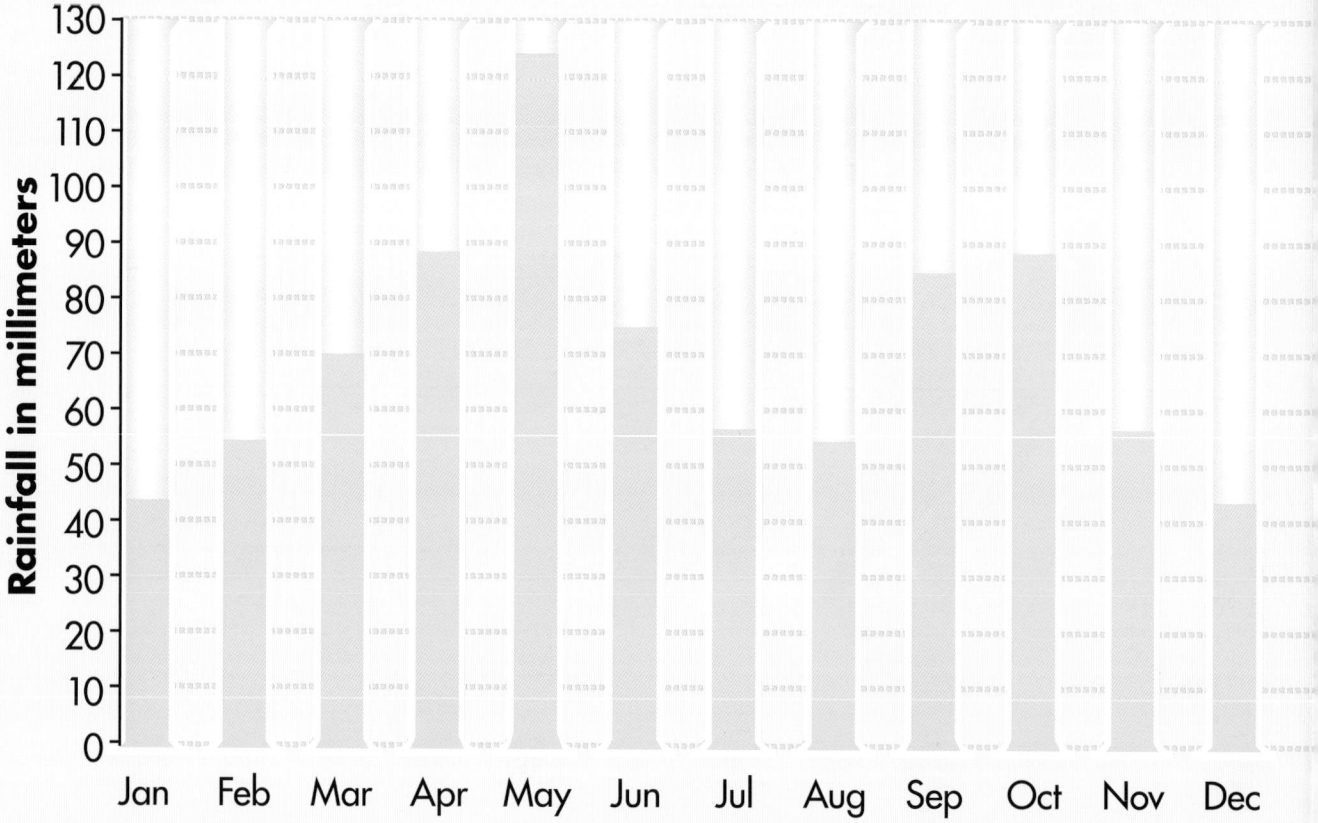

Temperature each month

This line graph shows the average temperature in Manchester, England, for each month for a year. It shows how the temperature rises and falls.

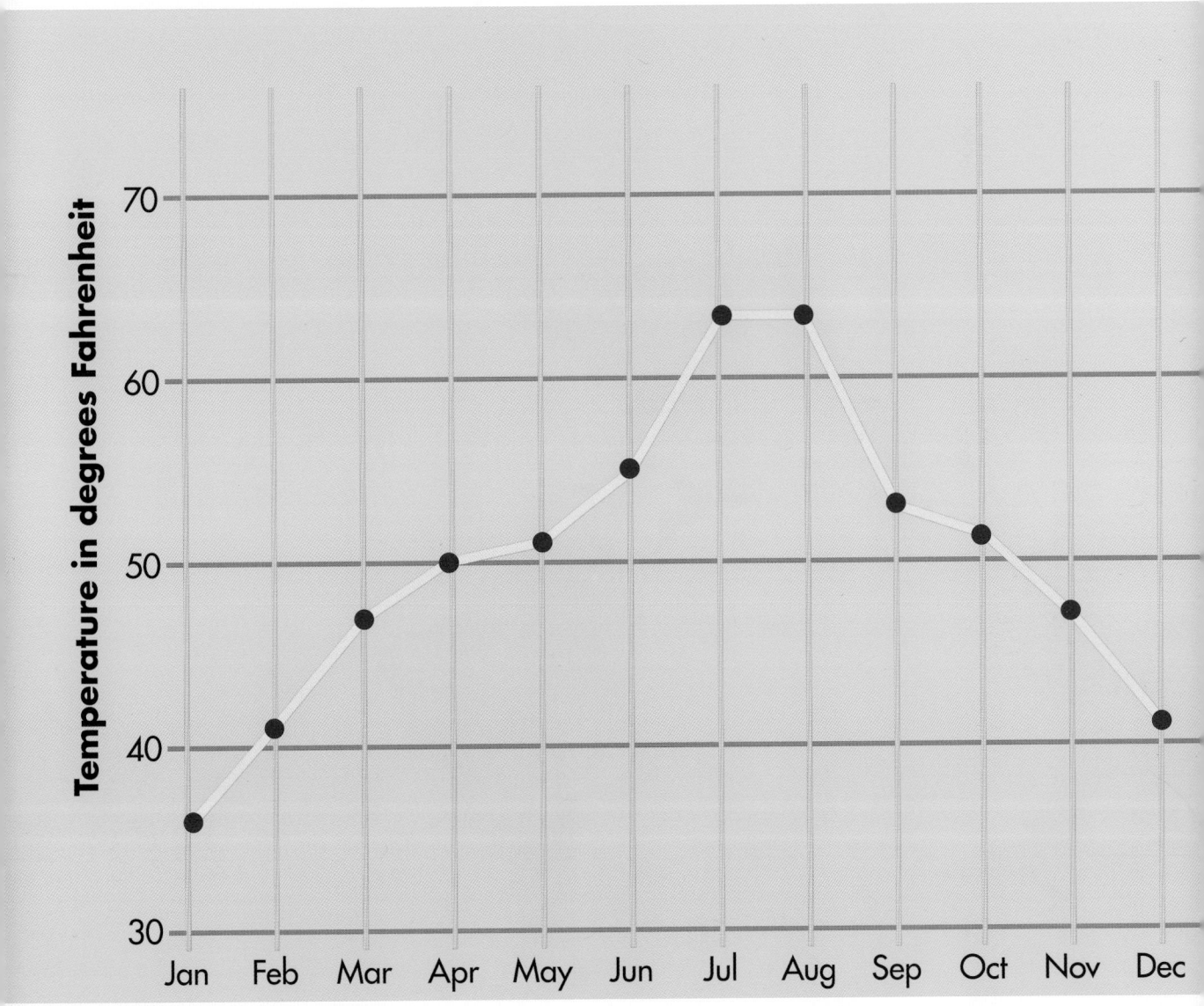

Climates around the world

This map shows what the climate is like in different parts of the world.

Polar very cold all year round

Temperate warm summers and cool winters

Desert very dry all year round

Tropical warm and rainy all year round

Mediterranean hot summers and warm winters

Mountains cold and snowy all year round

WEATHER FORECASTING

Weather forecasting means figuring out what the weather might be like for the next few days. This information is shown with weather maps. This is an example of a weather forecast map. You can see what weather will be like where you live.

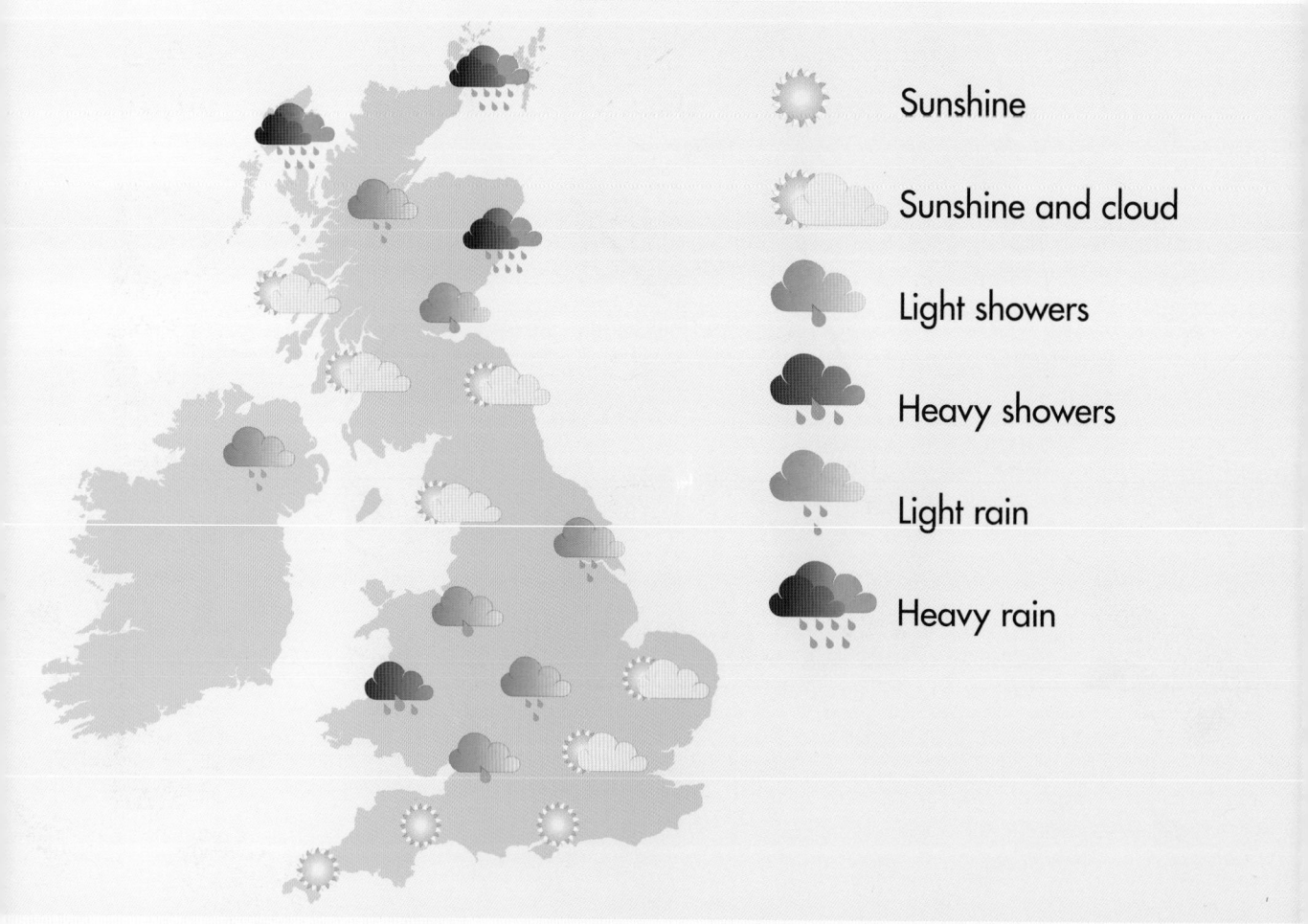

Weather for the week

This chart is an example of a five-day forecast. It shows in words and pictures what the weather will probably be like in the daytime for the next five days in a particular place.

Five-day forecast

Day	Weather	Max. Day (°F)	Min. Night (°F)	Wind (mph)
Mon		82	55	6
Tue		86	59	5
Wed		77	54	8
Thu		73	52	10
Fri		81	57	7

GLOSSARY

average sum of adding a set of numbers together and then dividing by the number of numbers in the set

calm not windy

climate pattern of weather that a place has over a long time

compass instrument for showing direction. A compass has a magnetic needle that points north.

lightning natural electricity produced in thunderclouds. Lightning appears as a bright flash or streak of light in the sky.

temperature how hot or cold something is

thunder booming noise that follows a flash of lightning

FIND OUT MORE

Books

Bodach, Vijaya. Making Graphs (series). Mankato, Minn.: Capstone, 2008.

Furgang, Kathy. *Everything Weather* (Everything). Washington, D.C.: National Geographic, 2012.

Ganeri, Anita. *Wild Weather* (Extreme Nature). Chicago: Raintree, 2013.

Web sites

Facthound offers a safe, fun way to find web sites related to this book. All the sites on Facthound have been researched by our staff.
Here's all you do:
Visit www.facthound.com
Type in this code: 9781410962195

INDEX

climates 24–27
clouds 16–17
cyclones 21

England 9, 25

five-day forecasts 5, 29

hail 12
hurricanes 20–21

infographics: what they are 4

lightning 18

rainfall 10–11, 24

snow 13
sunshine 15
symbols 6
temperatures 7, 8–9, 25
thunderstorms 18–19, 22
tornadoes 22–23
typhoons 21

United States 8, 12, 18, 23

weather forecasting 5, 28–29
weather maps 28
winds 14, 20, 22
world-record weather 7